URBAN GARDEN DESIGN

Private Terraces and Balconies

URBAN GARDEN DESIGN

Private Terraces and Balconies

Arboretum

LOFT

Editorial coordinator: Cristina Paredes

Texts: Xavier Bisbe, Ignasi Bisbe, Roser Vendrell

Art director: Mireia Casanovas Soley

Cover design: Claudia Martínez Alonso

Design: Emma Termes, Yolanda G. Román

Projects: Arboretum – www.arboretum.es

Images: Jordi Jové – www.jordi-jove.com

Styling: Conchita Crespo, Celi Colomer

English translation: Rachel Sarah Burden / Equipo de Edición

Copyediting and layout: Equipo de Edición

Editorial project:
2008 © LOFT Publications
Via Laietana 32, 4° Of. 92
08003 Barcelona, Spain
Tel.: +34 932 688 088
Fax: +34 932 687 073
loft@loftpublications.com
www.loftpublications.com

ISBN: 978-84-96936-29-4

Index

PURE EXTERIORISM

Landscape design, or landscape architecture, perfectly defines the projects presented in this work: the art of designing open spaces with living and inert elements as a way of transforming nature into an environment agreeable to humankind. The very etymology of the term for this discipline evokes a type of space that can be comprised by the view, shared by a community and used as a meeting forum in the urbanized fabric in which people live.

But when we get down to the details of residential landscapes, the term turns out to be frankly imprecise or incapable of expressing the initial complexity of a garden in a home.

I first heard the term 'exteriorism' in an informal conversation with Ignasi and Xavier Bisbe. It was the name the designers used to refer to a way of understanding their work, a viewpoint whereby factors such as privacy and family life (and even individual life) prevail over other considerations. It might be a limitation to the landscape and the landscape designer, but it is imposed in a positive sense and is capable of generating new experiences in the context of quotidian life. According to them, exteriorism means understanding a home's setting as just another of its inhabitable parts. It means extending the space that can be used and enjoyed through to the last corner of the garden or terrace. It incorporates the inside of a home with the garden and vice versa, creating an aesthetic dialogue between inside and outside that results in pure pleasure. It involves making designs in line with the necessary harmony between an apartment and its outdoor exit, or between a house and the land it sits on. And, of course, in terms of strict functionality.

Naturally, I asked to borrow the term and with their permission we have worked on it together, providing the satisfaction that comes from designating something which exists but lacks a name. The projects by Ignasi and Xavier Bisbe that illustrate this book are a fresh, living and contemporary illustration of what we understand as 'exteriorism'.

A leisurely look at their work, starting with the briefest, shows the affection and professionalism they apply to outdoor spaces with the aim of using every last inch to make another part of the home: gardens and balconies that can be used for pleasure throughout a large part of the year, if not year-round, and which also add a note of vitality and a breath of fresh air for whoever contemplates them from inside the home.

How do they do it? With good taste, a sense of proportion, visual purity, research into materials, respect for the environment, a mastery of spatial distribution and a profound knowledge of plant elements and the equipment available on the market to form an impeccable outdoor space.

I should also mention a further virtue of the good interior designer: an ability to listen to the customer and accomplish the spaces he identifies with and which meet his requirements to the tee. Behind the gardens and balconies that feature in this book and which were designed and built by Ignasi and Xavier Bisbe lies a drastic transformation to traditional landscape gardening that we have scarcely the perspective to perceive. But it is there. It is pure exteriorism.

Marcel Benedito
Editor, *Casa Viva* magazine
June 2007

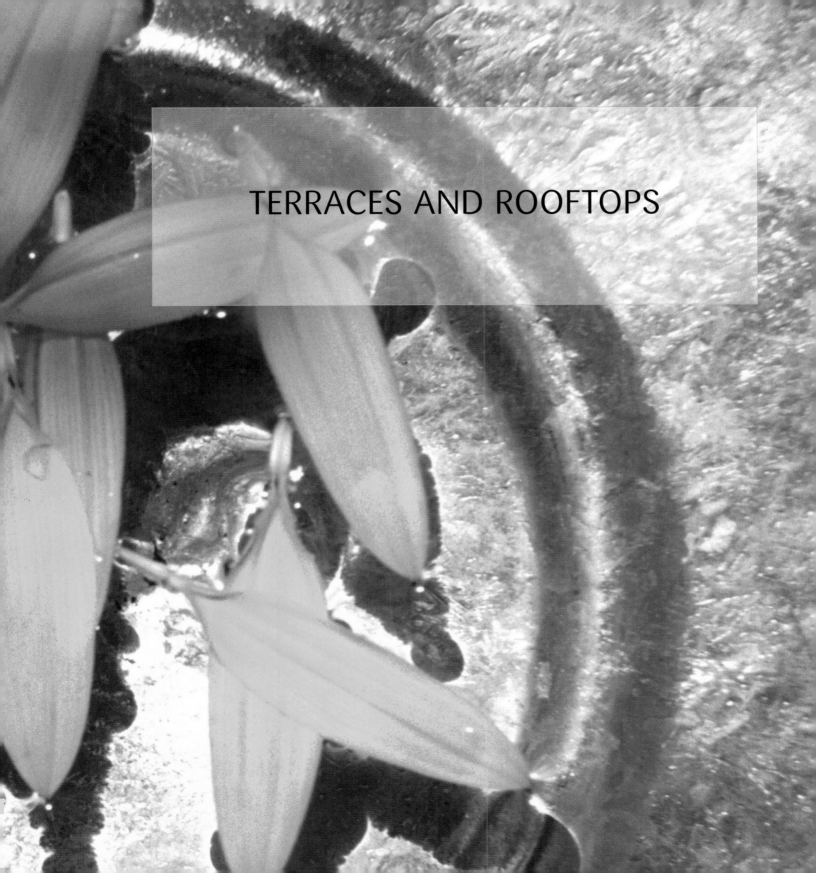

TERRACES AND ROOFTOPS

ROOF PARTY

This open rooftop, accessible from the apartment below, was landscaped to create a multifunctional space: a solarium by day and a party venue at night. The singularity of this project lay in the use of autochthonous and adapted low-maintenance plant species. The grass mats that protrude from the Brazilian walnut flooring, the pomegranate trees, aromatic plants and the cycas are characterized by their resistance to sharp changes in the weather and their ability to adapt to the harsh conditions of a completely uncovered urban terrace. The lighting, with stainless-steel lights embedded in the flooring, leads to the chill-out bench, from where you can enjoy a general view of the garden.

FLOOR TREATMENT: BRAZILIAN TROPICAL WALNUT FLOORING | **PLANT POTS AND PLANTER BOXES:** ZINC AND WOOD | **OUTDOOR FURNITURE:** CHILL-OUT BENCH WITH CUSHION AND THROW PILLOWS UPHOLSTERED IN MARINE-GRADE FABRIC | **PLANT SPECIES:** GRASS, POMEGRANATE TREES, AROMATIC PLANTS AND A CYCAS PLANT | **DECORATIVE OBJECTS:** GLASS VASES AND LIGHTS EMBEDDED IN THE FLOORING

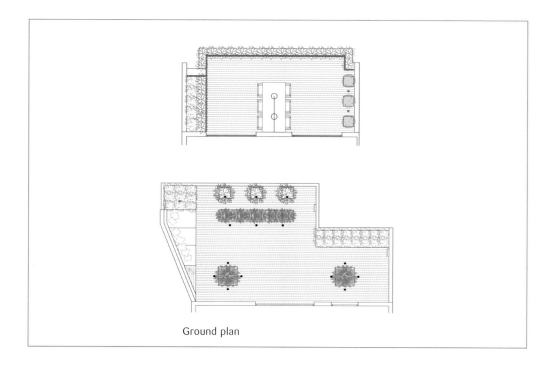

Ground plan

Because of the use the owner wanted to make of the space, the designer chose to make it completely diaphanous. The only thing that remains, on one side, is a large chill-out bed from which you can observe the whole of the landscaped rooftop. Trees planted in large zinc pots behind a grass mat in the flooring delimit a terrace whose altitude guarantees privacy. Because it was not necessary to prolong the wall with fencing, a feeling of continuity with the urban landscape is created, making an ideal space for a party.

IN A LOFT

The goal for the terrace of this city penthouse loft was to create continuity between the indoor living area and the outdoor space using Brazilian walnut flooring surrounded by marble stones. These give a new profundity and luminosity to the overall space, composed of three differentiated areas: the dining area, the living area and a solarium. A robust timber pergola shields the small living area (with wicker easy chairs, side table and chaise-longue) and the dining area. The solarium is reached via a walkway whose wooden planks change direction near the deck chairs to emphasize this area where a shower was also installed. The wall with stained pine fences to further increase privacy and the perimeter flower beds shore up the unity of the overall space.

FLOOR TREATMENT: BRAZILIAN WALNUT FLOORING AND MARBLE STONES | PLANT POTS AND PLANTER BOXES: EARTHENWARE AND WOOD | OUTDOOR FURNITURE: TWO WICKER EASY CHAIRS, SIDE TABLE AND CHAISE-LONGUE, DINING TABLE WITH TEAK TOP AND ALUMINUM BASE, CHAIRS WITH WICKER SEATS AND BACKS, TWO TIMBER DECK CHAIRS | PLANT SPECIES: CITRUS TREES, PALM TREE AND AROMATIC PLANTS | DECORATIVE OBJECTS: METAL VASE AND BOWLS, TABLE RUNNER AND CEILING LIGHTS, COMPLEMENTED BY EMBEDDED SPOTLIGHTS IN THE WALKWAY AND THE POTS TO ILLUMINATE THE TREES

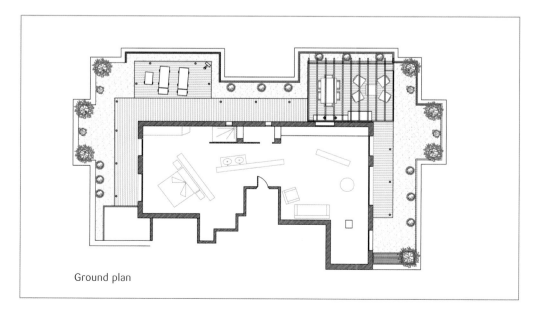

Ground plan

Because it is on the very top floor of the building, this terrace is bigger than the loft itself, which is why the idea was to complement a diaphanous interior space. A pergola with a timber base and dovetail joint planks, all in tropical-colored stained pine, completely covers the living and dining areas.

| A timber walkway with embedded spotlights to light it at night runs around the loft and terrace without covering the whole of the floor. The rest of the ground has been covered in marble stones. Plants and trees fill earthenware pots spread around the edge of the terrace. One only citrus tree, in a corner, has been planted in a timber pot, next to a bench of the same material.

HOTEL AMERICA

In downtown Barcelona, the Hotel America is a meeting point for executives and tourists from around the world. Management wanted to design the penthouse terrace so that guests could enjoy a morning dip or have a drink in a relaxed and sunny environment in the late afternoon. To ensure these activities that provide added-value service, it was organized into five zones: a living area, bar, solarium, chill-out space and a pool. To enjoy the sun and views, the designer chose not to build a fence above the wall but plant a string of lemon trees – an aromatic and essentially Mediterranean species – around the perimeter. The floor was laid with wood that would stand the weather, the water from the pool and the comings and goings of the people who would enjoy the terrace.

FLOOR TREATMENT: BRAZILIAN WALNUT FLOORING | **PLANT POTS AND PLANTER BOXES:** BROKEN-MOLDED POTS | **OUTDOOR FURNITURE:** HIGHLY RESISTANT ROTOMOLDED PLASTIC SOFAS NOT REQUIRING CUSHIONS, COFFEE TABLE, CHAIRS AND TABLES UNDER A PARASOL, DECK CHAIRS AND CHILL-OUT BED | **PLANT SPECIES:** LEMON TREES

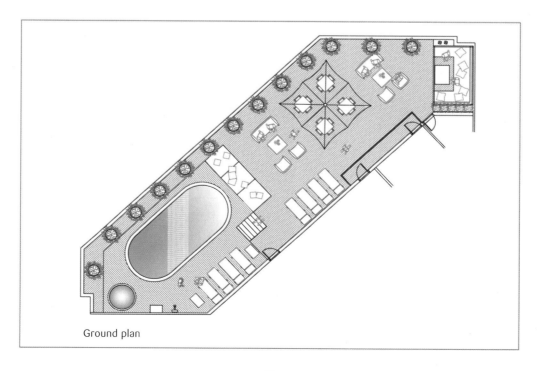

Ground plan

A medium-sized oval swimming pool was built at one end, on a timber platform reached from a flight of timber stairs with a shiny chrome tubular railing. Positioned around one end is a series of delicate deck chairs that leads to the living area, with rotomolded plastic sofas and a square coffee table.

A large parasol delimits the lunch-cum-bar area and at the other end, with a base of wooden planks and white seats with cushions, is the chill-out corner for chatting and listening to music. A large timber box hides the air-conditioning units and lighting is achieved via a succession of wall appliqués that surround the terrace.

CHILL-OUT SPACE

THE PURPOSE OF THIS PROJECT WAS TO MAKE A CHILL-OUT SPACE FOR A YOUNG WOMAN TO RELAX IN AND ENJOY. The balcony, which leads off the girl's bedroom and down to the garden with a pool, is covered in white for the 'Ibiza' look these spaces usually boast. A low, backless L-shaped bench, deeper than a sofa, runs around the perimeter and encloses the zone. The pure-white seats and cushions are coordinated with the screens, awnings and flower pots, while the touch of warmth comes from the coffee table and the Brazilian walnut flooring that paves and delimits the area. This outdoor living space is framed under a double timber pergola with straight walls and a canvas roof, providing maximum privacy to this outdoor space.

FLOOR TREATMENT: BRAZILIAN WALNUT FLOORING | PLANT POTS AND PLANTER BOXES: TERRACOTTA PAINTED WHITE | OUTDOOR FURNITURE: CHILL-OUT BENCH AND LOW COFFEE TABLE | PLANT SPECIES: BOXWOOD BALLS | DECORATIVE OBJECTS: SEATS UPHOLSTERED IN MARINE-GRADE FABRIC, CUSHIONS, BOTTLES FOR HOLDING CANDLES, FLOWER POT AND VASE

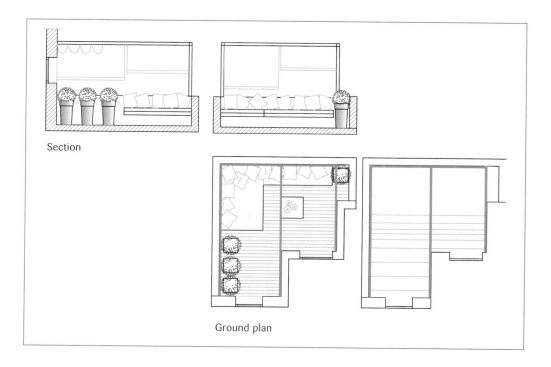

Section

Ground plan

The floor has been paved with Brazilian walnut, the same material used in the low coffee table, the height of which is just right for the custom-designed bench built for this space. A pergola with a timber structure, canvas awnings and screens ensures privacy and shields the space from the sun. The bright white seats and cushions – essential in a space like this – have been upholstered in marine-grade fabric for increased resistance. The turquoise bottles with candles form part of the decorative elements needed to create this type of ambiance.

DINING AREA WITH JACUZZI

TWO PERFECTLY DEFINED AREAS HAVE BEEN ORGANIZED ON THIS PENTHOUSE TERRACE: ONE FOR A SPA AREA AND THE OTHER FOR A DINING SPACE, UNITED BY A PASSAGEWAY WITH TREES. A large pergola has been installed at one of the main exits, with a canvas roof with cables that guide its opening by sections. At the end there is a bar with a sink and cupboards for use in the dining area, planter boxes around the perimeter and the original flooring. The passageway has been done up with a series of illuminated trees that lead to the second large outdoor area with Brazilian walnut flooring, a bench to relax on and a Jacuzzi on top of a raised platform. Next to the Jacuzzi, on the wooden floor, a rectangular hole has been made for a bed to be positioned flush with the floor. Here the fence has been raised to make the area more private.

FLOOR TREATMENT: BRAZILIAN WALNUT FLOORING AND NATURAL STONE | PLANT POTS AND PLANTER BOXES: TIMBER BOXES AND ZINC POTS | OUTDOOR FURNITURE: CUSTOM-MADE BENCHES AND TABLE WITH A METAL BASE AND TIMBER TOP, OUTDOOR CHAIRS AND A BAR WITH A SINK | PLANT SPECIES: SHRUBS, AROMATIC PLANTS, BAMBOO CANE AND LEMON TREES | DECORATIVE OBJECTS: VASES, CANDLES AND SPOTLIGHTS

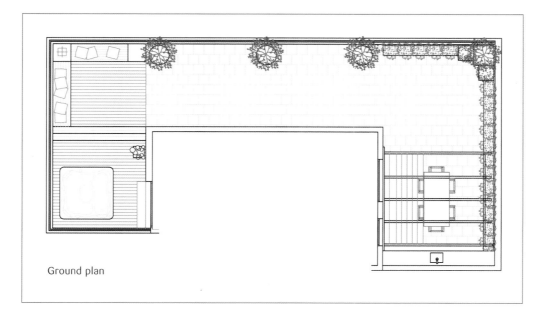

Ground plan

The two zones are connected by an illuminated path of trees. The spa area is paved with tropical wood, perfect for putting around swimming pools and spa baths as it is resistant to moisture and less slippery. In the dining area, the bar attached to the wall that separates this property from that of the neighbors is particularly interesting: it includes storage drawers and a sink for use in this diaphanous dining space.

CHILL-OUT SPACE WITH SOLARIUM

THIS PROJECT INVOLVED THE CONSTRUCTION OF A VERY COMPLETE CHILL-OUT SPACE WITH A SOLARIUM. It is on the second floor of a duplex apartment and is accessed via a studio. A pergola with an aluminum base, covered with an awning and side screens, delimits the meeting and relaxation area composed of a u-shaped sofa that encourages conversation. The living area – slightly raised to set it apart from the rest of the terrace – is finished with a coffee table. In front of this, a landscaped solarium with a pair of aluminum deck chairs with special outdoor screen fabric adds a new use to the site. The wood flooring only covers part of the floor; for the rest, marble stones add light and another dimension.

FLOOR TREATMENT: BRAZILIAN WALNUT FLOORING AND MARBLE STONESS | **PLANT POTS AND PLANTER BOXES:** CHOCOLATE BROWN BROKEN-MOLDED POTS | **OUTDOOR FURNITURE:** SOFA-BED WITH CUSHIONS AND BACKS UPHOLSTERED IN MARINE-GRADE FABRIC, COFFEE TABLE AND TWO DECK CHAIRS | **PLANT SPECIES:** CITRUS AND OLIVE TREES | **DECORATIVE OBJECTS:** GLASS JARS AND SPOTLIGHTS IN THE POTS TO ILLUMINATE THE TREES

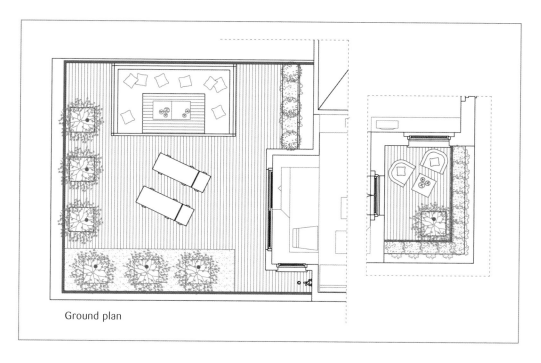

Ground plan

| Citrus and olive trees are planted right around the perimeter to delimit the terrace from the studio and further enhance the privacy which the stained pinewood fences on top of the walls provide. The chill-out zone is custom-made for the space, on a small u-shaped stage. In the background, a wall with the same Brazilian walnut as used on the floor achieves an optimal vision of the whole. The delicate pergola with white screens is perfect for achieving the desired chill-out look.

INSPIRATION: MARRAKECH

Open diamond latticework, a table with a ceramic mosaic top, reed curtains, a fountain and candles define this space with Arabian touches. To make sure it did not look too exaggerated, all the elements maintain a certain ethnic air, but are fairly restrained. The summer dining area is located beneath a timber pergola with a canvas top and roll-up wicker curtains at the front and side. To the right, a service area has been closed off with a pair of mobile lattice frames, between which a custom-designed flat fountain was installed. Separated by a change in the direction of paving on the original terrazzo, an open area can be used for sunbathing. The whole of the terrace was enclosed with a latticework of large diamonds and a planter box along the wall to even out the slope of the ground.

FLOOR TREATMENT: PINEWOOD FLOORING AT THE SAME LEVEL AS THE OTHER HALF WITH THE ORIGINAL PAVING | PLANT POTS AND PLANTER BOXES: PINEWOOD | OUTDOOR FURNITURE: TABLE WITH TIMBER BASE AND CERAMIC TOP AND TEAK CHAIRS | PLANT SPECIES: BOXWOOD CUT INTO BALL SHAPES AND CREEPER PLANTS | DECORATIVE OBJECTS: CANDLE LAMP, TABLE RUNNER, BOWLS AND FOUNTAIN

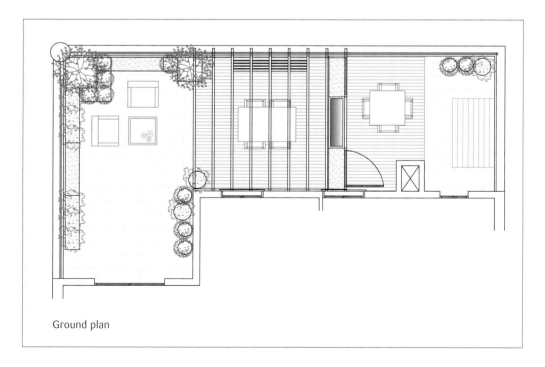

Ground plan

The purpose of this project was to transform a conventional urban terrace into a Mediterranean courtyard with a certain Arabic air. To prevent a sharp contrast between the city landscape and this space, lattices were used to semi-hide the terrace. Its main use is as a summer dining area, so the pergola, table and chairs, set on Brazilian walnut flooring, are the focus of attention. The change in paving was done to distinguish zones and the fountain acts as a wall that conceals the laundry room.

ROOF GARDEN

This garden is located on the roof of a modern home close to the sea. The owner wanted a terrace garden that would provide a sharp contrast with the indoor spaces. The main work involved the landscape gardening: timber planter boxes were alternated with terracotta pots filled with leafy species of Mediterranean essence. The outdoor space is reached via an arbor which communicates the property, below, with this garden divided into two zones: the solarium with a shower and the summer dining area, with furniture of an aluminum base and timber bodies and parasol with an adjustable arm. Timber walls enhance the privacy of some areas and others are concealed behind plants that act as a scenic backdrop.

FLOOR TREATMENT: BRAZILIAN WALNUT FLOORING | PLANT POTS AND PLANTER BOXES: TIMBER PLANTER BOXES AND TERRACOTTA POTS | OUTDOOR FURNITURE: DECK CHAIRS, TABLE AND CHAIRS WITH A METAL BASE AND TIMBER BODIES | PLANT SPECIES: MIXTURE OF MULTIPLE AND VARIED MEDITERRANEAN PLANT SPCIES | DECORATIVE OBJECTS: GARDEN SHOWER, OFF-CENTER AWNING, GLASS VASE AND WICKER TRAY

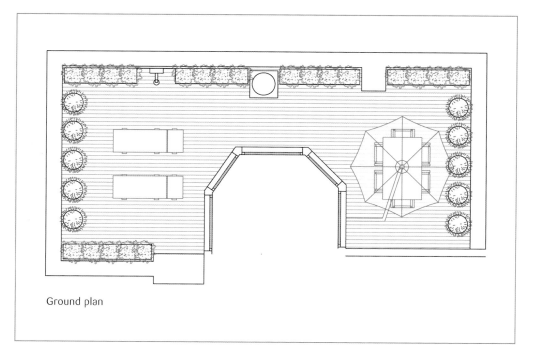

Ground plan

| The reorganization of this leafy Mediterranean garden involved arduous work in perimeter landscape gardening, with timber planter boxes continued with walls of the same material. The open areas of the terrace feature terracotta pots filled with trees and high bushes. The shower installed here is more typical of a garden than a terrace.

WINTER LIVING SPACE

THE PURPOSE OF THIS PROJECT WAS TO CREATE AN INDOOR AREA IN AN EXTERIOR SPACE. To prolong the home's living areas, a timber structure was built with an asphalt tile roof and glass walls, where the light is filtered by the use of screens that frame this winter living space. The same parquet is used in the covered area as on the terrace, causing a feeling of continuity. The outside area, with Brazilian walnut flooring and planter boxes around the perimeter, is devoted to an open solarium. At the end, a timber shed functions as a storage space. At the exit of the winter living area, which can be opened up and also used in summer, are five terracotta pots with flowers, making this special part of the terrace warm and cheerful.

FLOOR TREATMENT: PARQUET AND BRAZILIAN WALNUT FLOORING | PLANT POTS AND PLANTER BOXES: WOOD BOXES AND TERRACOTTA POTS | OUTDOOR FURNITURE: WICKER SOFA WITH UPHOLSTERED SEATS, A PAIR OF TIMBER COFFEE TABLES, A BOOKSHELF, ARMCHAIR, FLOOR LAMP AND DECK CHAIR | PLANT SPECIES: SHRUBS, AROMATIC PLANTS, LEMON TREE AND FLOWERS | DECORATIVE OBJECTS: PAINTINGS, VASE, COFFEE TABLE AND SCREENS IN THE WINTER AREA; METAL BUCKET AND CUSHIONS ON THE OUTDOOR TERRACE

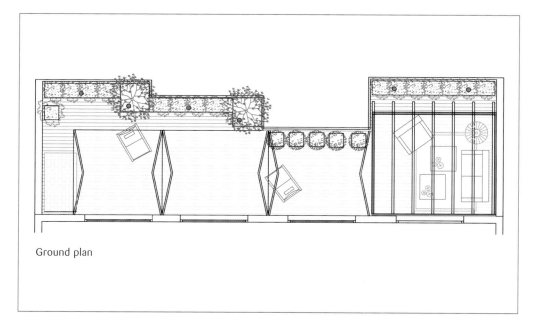

Ground plan

The warm decoration of this winter living area has been totally coordinated with the interior design of the home's living room so as to create not a separate zone but a logical continuation of the living area. While the flowering plants that adorn the exit of the living area have been planted in terracotta pots, the other plants and trees are planted in Brazilian walnut boxes and hide the balcony rails, creating a compact effect for the open solarium.

TRANSFORMATION WITH CHARM

THIS PENTHOUSE TERRACE HAD A STONE FLOOR THAT WAS ON A SLOPE AND HAD SEEN BETTER DAYS, PLANTS POSITIONED LISTLESSLY IN A ROW, A PAIR OF REGULAR AWNINGS AND PLASTIC FURNITURE. To bring charm to a previously impersonal outdoor area, Brazilian walnut flooring was used to even out the ground and make the floor look warmer. A timber pergola with a canvas awning was built at the main exit, reaching right to the end of the balcony. Beneath this are a spacious dining area – now with comfortable teak furniture – and a pre-existing custom-made barbeque which separates the space from the neighbors via a timber fence. The open southern side is for enjoying the view. A compact perimeter planter box of continental Mediterranean plants unifies the whole area.

FLOOR TREATMENT: BRAZILIAN WALNUT FLOORING | PLANT POTS AND PLANTER BOXES: TREATED AND STAINED PINEWOOD | OUTDOOR FURNITURE: TEAK TABLE, CHAIRS, DECK CHAIRS AND SIDE TABLE | PLANT SPECIES: LAVENDER, BOXWOOD AND OTHER SPECIES FROM THE CONTINENTAL MEDITERRANEAN FAMILY OR INDOOR PLANTS THAT BEST SUPPORT LOW TEMPERATURES | DECORATIVE OBJECTS: BARBEQUE, SCULPTURE, OUTDOOR SHOWER AND THROW PILLOWS

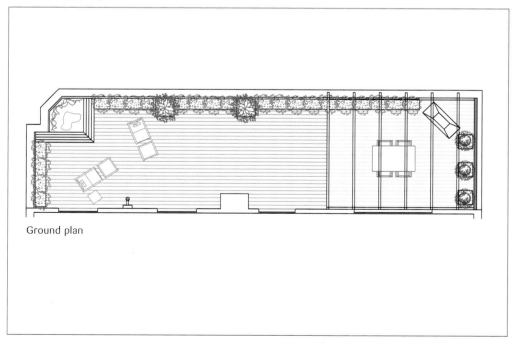

Ground plan

The before-and-after shots show what the terrace looked like previously, and the warmer and more personal aspect it has now, thanks to the Brazilian walnut flooring and the compact perimeter planter box made from stained pinewood. The awnings were replaced by a pergola with a canvas awning that also protects the northern end. On the other side, a solarium zone with an outdoor shower, deck chairs and a sculpture half-surrounded by a custom-made table make a pleasant living corner.

URBAN PENTHOUSE

WHEN REVAMPING THE TERRACE OF THIS STUDIO LOCATED ON THE TOP FLOOR OF A TALL BUILDING, THE DESIGNERS TOOK INTO ACCOUNT THAT THE PROPRIETOR'S LIFESTYLE INVOLVES CONSTANT TRAVEL. To maintain a practical and minimalist style, only essential plants were placed in strategic points in this generous outdoor area. The interior is closely linked with the spacious terrace that prolongs the living room in terms of views and light. An opaque fence made from timber walls and latticework runs around the perimeter. The tropical wood flooring does not extend right to the end at the front or at one of the sides in order to play with the depth: white stones add a touch of light and break the continuity of the boards. A rectangular table and a pair of benches conform the summer dining area.

FLOOR TREATMENT: BRAZILIAN WALNUT FLOORING AND WHITE STONES | PLANT POTS AND PLANTER BOXES: BLACK ZINC POTS | OUTDOOR FURNITURE: TABLE AND BENCHES | PLANT SPECIES: POMEGRANATE TREE AND BOXWOOD BALLS | DECORATIVE OBJECTS: TABLE RUNNER AND DINNER SERVICE

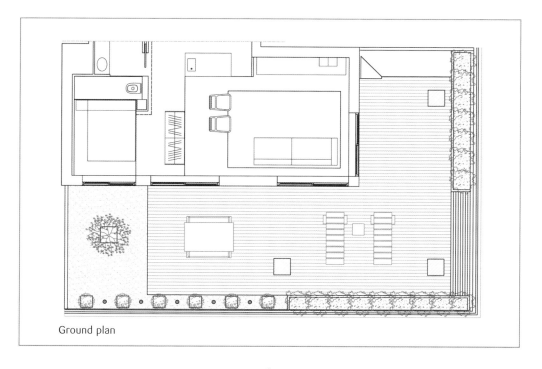

Ground plan

Halogen spotlights were embedded in the floor among the white crushed stones between the plants to make the area look particularly inviting at night. The plants in the planter boxes are low-maintenance. The table and benches parallel to the indoor dining area are made from a metal base and wooden boards, with a very contemporary design involving straight and refined lines. The end with the best views has been fitted with a latticework that acts as a wall and next to it there is a bench with throw pillows.

SUITE TERRACE

THIS TERRACE IS LOCATED ON THE THIRD FLOOR OF A FAMILY HOME. It is a garden attached to the main bedroom suite and is characterized by its personal and exclusive style. To create a walkway with piped music between the trees, the path was marked with long wooden boards that do not reach the sides. Between the L-shaped Brazilian walnut platform and the wall of the terrace, large pot plants with trees and plants have been positioned on white stones. The central walkway, marked with LED lights, reaches an independent stainless-steel fountain sculpture. To complete the scene and take advantage of the property's home-automation technology, here too there are amplifiers along certain parts of the path to enjoy the piped music.

FLOOR TREATMENT: BRAZILIAN WALNUT FLOORING AND WHITE STONES | PLANT POTS AND PLANTER BOXES: ZINC, TERRACOTTA AND ANTHRACITE GLAZED EARTHENWARE POTS | PLANT SPECIES: MANDARIN TREES, BOXWOOD BALLS, FICUS AND MACRO BONSAIS | DECORATIVE OBJECTS: LED LIGHTS INSTALLED IN THE WOOD FLOORING AND A STAINLESS-STEEL FOUNTAIN

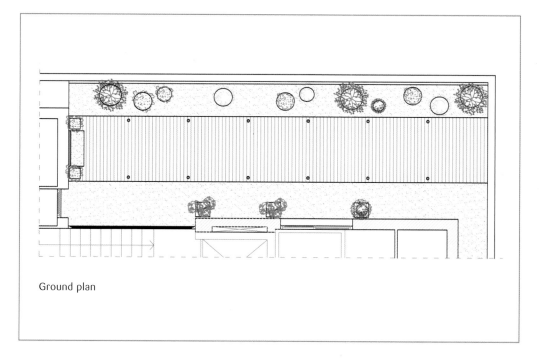

Ground plan

Two macro bonsais planted in large zinc pots flank the bedroom window. No furniture has been used, because the function of this space is purely aesthetic and to walk through. Supported on one of the walls and between two boxwood plants, the stainless-steel undulating fountain sculpture, the work of an English artist, decorates the garden. This outdoor space runs around the front of the top floor and affords pleasant views from the bedroom.

MEDITERRANEAN ESSENCE

LOCATED IN A PENTHOUSE WITH SPECTACULAR VIEWS OVER THE CITY OF BARCELONA AND FACING THE SEA, THIS LOVELY, PEACEFUL TERRACE IS CHARACTERIZED BY ITS ELONGATED SHAPE. This meant the different areas to redesign had to be arranged along the length of the terrace, in line with the different indoor rooms of the apartment. Firstly come a summer outdoor-dining space and solarium – both under roll-up awnings – and then the corner used as a living space, shielded by a glass-roofed timber pergola. These elements filled the terrace with vitality and made it a very flexible space. Another clever idea was to temper the city views with green vegetation that still lets abundant light in.

FLOOR TREATMENT: BRAZILIAN WALNUT FLOORING | PLANT POTS AND PLANTER BOXES: TERRACCOTA AND WOOD | OUTDOOR FURNITURE: TEAK TABLE, CHAIRS, DECK CHAIRS AND SIDE TABLES | PLANT SPECIES: OLIVE TREES AND LAUREL BUSHES | DECORATIVE OBJECTS: WHITE TABLE RUNNER, GLASS VASE, CANDLES, THROW PILLOWS

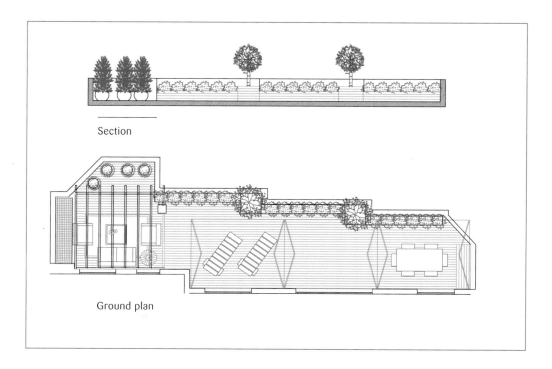

Section

Ground plan

| The Brazilian walnut flooring is extended in the living space with a bench with a vent at the bottom for the air-conditioning unit. The flooring gives uniformity to the three ambiances, whose harmony can be observed when seen as a whole. The dining area and solarium are positioned under roll-up awnings and the living space is under a timber pergola with a glass safety roof. The chaotic view of buildings is semi-hidden by timber flower pots planted with typically Mediterranean trees and shrubs that end at the living space, where large terracotta flower pots are used instead.

MINIMALIST SPIRIT

This large balcony surrounds the front part of the first floor of an urban building and looks onto a busy street. Recovering it for domestic life has brought a new meaning to this privileged space that until it was done up was not being used and had very little privacy because of its proximity to the public road. To shield it from outsiders and reintegrate it with the home, structures made from Brazilian walnut boards were built around the perimeter. The central area was left completely clear for the children of the home to run around in freely. The decorative contribution was limited to a succession of pot plants filled with species of large trees and aromatic plants. The continuity of the perimeter landscaping is broken by the use of benches with cushions and throw pillows.

FLOOR TREATMENT: BRAZILIAN WALNUT FLOORING | PLANT POTS AND PLANTER BOXES: WALNUT STAINED AND TREATED WOOD | OUTDOOR FURNITURE: BENCHES AND FOLDING SIDE TABLE | PLANT SPECIES: OLIVE TREES, POMEGRANATE TREE, CITRUS TREES, ROSEMARY AND LAVENDER PLANTS | DECORATIVE OBJECTS: OFF-WHITE CUSHIONS, BOWLS AND VASES

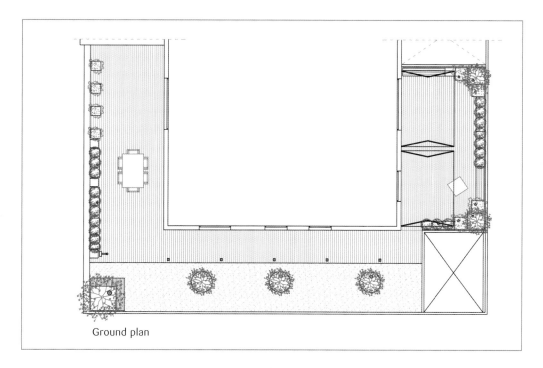

Ground plan

The floor of the terrace was evened out with tropical Brazilian walnut flooring, the same material used for the vertical perimeter structure which shields the space from the bustling street. Few and very carefully chosen elements were positioned around the edges to leave a generous and uncluttered central space: a couple of benches and timber pot plants filled with trees and small plants of Mediterranean essence. The minimalist spirit of this project made it possible to isolate the terrace from the grim exterior while respecting its recreational function.

INDEPENDENT SPACE

THE CHALLENGE FOR THIS OUTDOOR SPACE, LOCATED ON THE ROOFTOP OF A TALL BUILDING AND ACCESSED VIA AN INTERNAL STAIRWAY IN THE PENTHOUSE, WAS TO OBTAIN A DYNAMIC ENVIRONMENT PACKED WITH LIFE AND WHICH WAS COMPLETELY INDEPENDENT: A RELAXATION ZONE PROTECTED FROM THE SUN, RAIN AND CURIOUS EYES. The concept of independence led to the design of a buffet with an integrated fridge, a tap with running water and a cupboard. No detail was spared to ensure the complete use and enjoyment of the area, including a children's wading pool, a shower and a large chill-out area under a pergola with a dovetail joint roof, all in stained and treated pinewood, with finishes and weatherproofing in roofing shingles. From the terrace you can see the living area of the floor below, with views over the city and articulated around wicker easy chairs with a small coffee table in the middle.

FLOOR TREATMENT: BRAZILIAN TROPICAL WALNUT FLOORING AND CRUSHED STONES | PLANT POTS AND PLANTER BOXES: TERRACOTTA PAINTED WHITE | OUTDOOR FURNITURE: CHILL-OUT BENCH WITH CUSHION AND THROW PILLOWS UPHOLSTERED IN MARINE-GRADE FABRIC, BRAZILIAN WALNUT BAR WITH BLACK GRANITE TOP, COFFEE TABLE AND WICKER EASY CHAIRS | PLANT SPECIES: BOXWOOD BALLS AND SHRUBS | DECORATIVE OBJECTS: WICKER BASKET, TRAY, GLASS VASE AND LANTERN

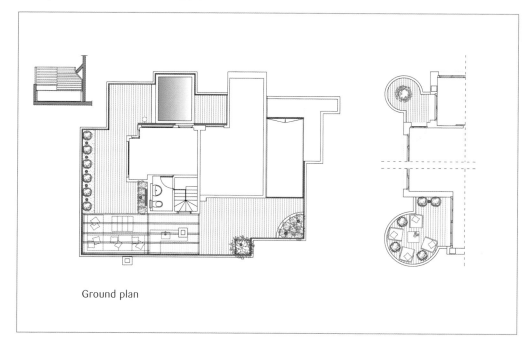

Ground plan

The zinc pots with boxwood balls were positioned on a perimeter path of white stones, where spotlights illuminate the plants around the edges of the terrace. On top of the walls, a dark-timber gapped fence conceals the living area and swimming pool.

The creation of a warm and comfortable space decided the choice of a noble material like timber for the arbor and chill-out areas, designed and built to measure. The exposed brick wall opposite the bar features a fountain with a mirrored surface which is operated independently and adds a very relaxing sound of flowing water.

LITTLE PARADISE IN THE CITY

This downtown attic terrace is a garden among tall buildings, perfect for spending pleasant hours eating and enjoying the sun. To create privacy, the wall was covered in Brazilian walnut wood, in line with the flooring, and crowned with a gapped timber fence. The dining area is located under a pergola with a stained pine structure and a glass roof to allow the natural light in from overhead. The solarium is completely open and features a delicate deck chair with wheels. The flooring is broken up with a strip of marble stones that add light and depth to the overall look. The plant pots were positioned on the floor along the front and provide a leafy background that semi-conceals the city views.

FLOOR TREATMENT: BRAZILIAN WALNUT FLOORING AND MARBLE STONES | PLANT POTS AND PLANTER BOXES: ZINC AND WOOD | OUTDOOR FURNITURE: TABLE WITH A TIMBER TOP AND ALUMINUM STRUCTURE, FOUR CHAIRS WITH SCREEN-FABRIC BACKS AND SEATS, DECK CHAIR WITH REAR WHEELS AND CUSTOM-MADE TIMBER BENCH | PLANT SPECIES: BOXWOOD BALLS, BONSAI AND SHRUBS | DECORATIVE OBJECTS: TABLE RUNNER, GLASS VASES, BENCH CUSHION AND SPOTLIGHTS IN THE PERGOLA

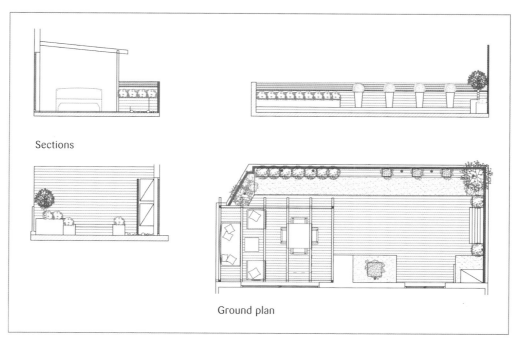

Sections

Ground plan

| A large rectangular planter box was positioned in the living area, filled with jungle-style plants to make the eating area more private. The solarium features a succession of three high pots with boxwood balls that do not block the sun but add a more rational look that contrasts with the other corners. At the end, a small bench attached to the high timber wall that separates this terrace from that of the neighbors makes a corner in which to relax after enjoying the sun.

PENTHOUSE WITH VIEWS

This terrace pertains to a penthouse of more than 4,000 square feet with excellent views over the city. Located in a noble building, the façade on this side of the property has an arbor that makes one end of the space very exclusive and was the object chosen to emphasize. The space is designed as a relaxation area for friends and a place to enjoy evening parties in two areas: a summer dining room that seats ten or more people and a relaxation area for having a drink, with a buffet and garden. To properly delimit the different zones, the designers played with the flooring, respecting the original terrazzo and using floorboards for the living areas. A pergola in each zone shores up the distinction and protects the spaces from the weather.

FLOOR TREATMENT: BRAZILIAN WALNUT FLOORING AND ORIGINAL TERRAZZO | **PLANT POTS AND PLANTER BOXES:** ZINC POTS | **OUTDOOR FURNITURE:** TABLE, TEN CHAIRS, BUFFET, TWO EASY CHAIRS, ALL IN TEAK MASONITE® | **PLANT SPECIES:** POMEGRANATE, LEMON, MANDARIN AND OLIVE TREES, LAUREL AND OTHER MEDITERRANEAN PLANTS | **DECORATIVE OBJECTS:** CUSHIONS, CANDLES, VASES, FRUIT PLATTERS AND TABLE RUNNER

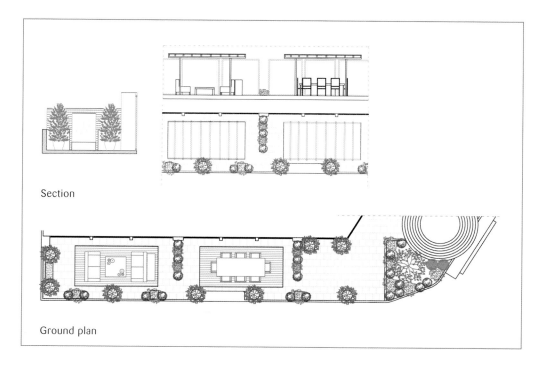

Section

Ground plan

The living areas on this terrace are protected by the use of two treated and stained Brazilian walnut pergolas which are very solid despite their delicate aspect, with a double-glazing roof and an intermediate layer of vinyl. The furniture is made from teak Masonite® and the planter boxes stand out for their Mediterranean essence, with autochthonous plants and leafy fruit trees, as the bold design permits them.

The outdoor chill-out space is composed of two large two-seat sofas facing each other with a decorated coffee table in-between. The large dining table can seat ten and is illuminated by two hanging lights.

BALCONIES

A BALCONY ONTO THE PARK

THIS URBAN GARDEN-DESIGN PROJECT, CARRIED OUT ON A FAIRLY SMALL BALCONY, WAS COMPLETELY CONDITIONED BY ITS LOCATION: A HIGH-LEVEL APARTMENT WITH VIEWS OVER AN IMPRESSIVE PARK. To emphasize this privileged setting, the medium-height rail was left untouched, with wooden planks used at the bottom and the top made from glass with no further ornamentation. The spectacular views are the focus of all the attention, so the terrace was designed to act as an outdoor living area that faces the garden, an intermediate space between the house and the leafy park. To enjoy the silence and the views, a number of elements were added to the living space, including a pair of easy chairs, between which was positioned a sofa, some wicker pouffes and decorative complements that give the balcony a cheerful touch.

FLOOR TREATMENT: BRAZILIAN TEAKWOOD FLOORING | **PLANT POTS AND PLANTER BOXES:** ZINC AND WICKER; POT FOR LEMON TREE, MODEL 'LECHUZA' | **OUTDOOR FURNITURE:** EASY CHAIRS WITH WICKER STRUCTURE, SOFA WITH SPECIAL OUTDOOR COVER, WICKER POUFFES | **PLANT SPECIES:** LEMON TREE AND THUNBERGIAS | **DECORATIVE OBJECTS:** WHITE AND OFF-WHITE SEATS AND CUSHIONS, FLOOR LAMP, LARGE CANDLE, BOWLS AND WICKER BASKET/PLANT POT

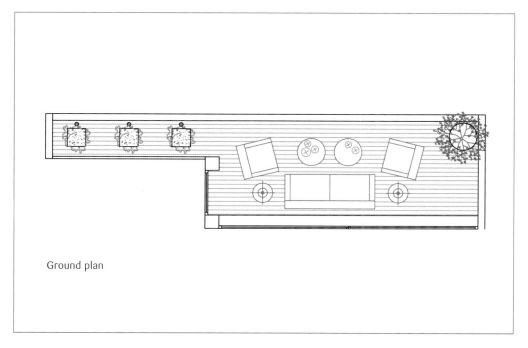

Ground plan

| The balcony has been paved with Brazilian teakwood flooring, lighter than walnut and which does not darken over time. The same material covers the bottom of the balcony up to the transparent railing, heightening the sense of continuity. The three zinc pots, positioned in a row at the narrowest part of the balcony, are medium height, in line with the timber base of the balcony, and the small-flowered thunbergias poke out just enough to not block the view of the park.

| In the living area, two easy chairs and a sofa are complemented by a pair of wicker pouffes – used as seats or footrests – and coffee tables. Here there is a single lemon tree strategically placed in the corner to decorate the timber wall that separates this apartment from that of the neighbors.

URBAN GARDEN DESIGN WITHOUT PLANTS

THIS OUTDOOR LIVING AREA IS AN EXAMPLE OF URBAN GARDEN DESIGN CARRIED OUT PRACTICALLY WITH NO PLANTS OF ANY TYPE. Because it is a small and relatively narrow balcony, the designers opted for a minimalist look to make a living area with straight-line furniture and few ornaments. As the space is located opposite a large public park, the idea was to avoid overdoing it with plants that would block the splendid views. The floor and façade wall were covered with Brazilian walnut wood to achieve continuity and a compact view of the whole, perfect for a small space like this. The furniture is neutral and its subtle presence does not compete with the true star of the show: the backdrop, which monopolizes all the attention and is the raison d'être of this balcony.

FLOOR TREATMENT: BRAZILIAN WALNUT FLOORING | **PLANT POTS AND PLANTER BOXES:** BLACK ZINC POTS | **OUTDOOR FURNITURE:** BRAIDED SYNTHETIC FIBER SOFA AND EASY CHAIRS, ALUMINUM COFFEE TABLE WITH TOBACCO-COLORED POLYETHYLENE AND A STOOL USED AS A SIDE TABLE | **PLANT SPECIES:** BOXWOOD BALLS AND A PAIR OF SCHEFFLERA PLANTS | **DECORATIVE OBJECTS:** GLASS VASE, WATER JUG, GLASSES AND CANDLES

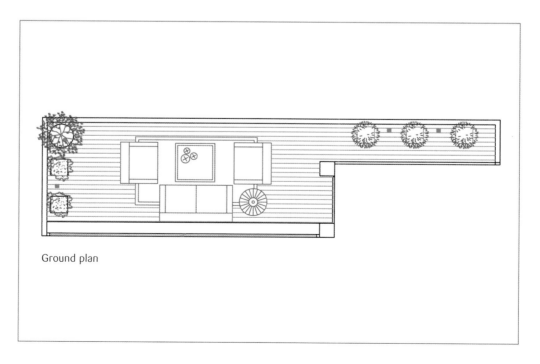

Ground plan

This is a refined balcony, completely coordinated with the landscape, which is the true star. There are just a couple of plant species in strategic spots that help conceal the wall that separates this home from the neighbors' and which are covered in wood. Two schefflera plants in black zinc pots and a row of boxwood balls along the narrowest part of the balcony decorate the low zone of this showcase for the inside of the apartment.

SMALL PRIVATE PARADISE

THE IDEA FOR THIS BALCONY WAS TO CREATE A WELCOMING AND PLANT-FILLED SHOW-CASE FOR THE INSIDE OF THE APARTMENT AND TO PROTECT IT FROM BEING SEEN FROM THE BLOCKS IN FRONT AND FROM THE NOISE FROM THE STREET. Brazilian walnut flooring was laid and a first row of planter boxes built, along with a custom-made fountain. Next to the balcony wall, a second row of timber planter boxes with jungle-style plants forms a type of curtain, an idea shored up by the addition of vertical awnings. An outdoor living space with wicker furniture and a colonial-style table; an exotic walkway with an illuminated Zen fountain, two circular flower pots and a birdcage; a bench with a cushion and a pair of wicker easy chairs complete this small private paradise in the city.

FLOOR TREATMENT: BRAZILIAN WALNUT FLOORING | PLANT POTS AND PLANTER BOXES: CUSTOM-MADE TIMBER PLANTER BOXES | OUTDOOR FURNITURE: SOFA AND WICKER EASY CHAIRS, COFFEE TABLE, FLOOR LAMP, SIDE TABLE, TIMBER BENCH WITH CUSHION AND DARK WICKER EASY CHAIRS | PLANT SPECIES: MIX OF MANY VARIED JUNGLE-STYLE PLANT SPECIES | DECORATIVE OBJECTS: VASES, COFFEE TABLES, ILLUMINATED CUSTOM-MADE FOUNTAIN AND BIRDCAGE

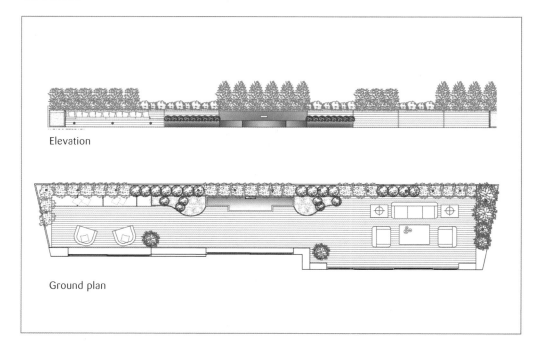

Elevation

Ground plan

THE SHOWCASE BALCONY

THIS PROJECT IS BASED ON A STANDARD NARROW BALCONY WHICH HAS BEEN GIVEN THE FUNCTION OF A SHOWCASE FOR THE LIVING AND DINING ROOMS OF THE APARTMENT. Because the views are not attractive, the balcony acquires a radically different use by prolonging the living areas and taking them outdoors via a pair of cubes made from fixed glass. This enables the house to invade the balcony and provides a minimum outdoor space that complements the indoor areas and acts as a backdrop to the expanded daytime zones of the property. The decoration is neutral and respects the coordination of the prevailing tones and styles of the apartment to harmonize both ambiances. It backs onto the street and all the attention centers on the inhabitable spaces: a good example of a decorative balcony with practical touches.

FLOOR TREATMENT: CERAMIC FLOOR TILES | **PLANT POTS AND PLANTER BOXES:** BEHIND A STRUCTURE COVERED IN HIGH-TECH WOOD | **OUTDOOR FURNITURE:** BENCHES WITH METAL LEGS AND HIGH-TECH WOOD SEATS, COMPOSED OF 70% WOOD AND 30% RESIN | **PLANT SPECIES:** BOXWOOD BALLS | **DECORATIVE OBJECTS:** WHITE AND BROWN CUSHIONS

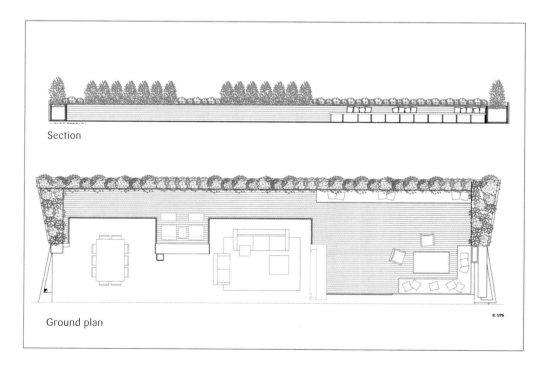

Section

Ground plan

E: 1/75

The balcony is blocked off from the outside via vertical blinds that are lowered when privacy is required or raised to let the natural light in. The walls and benches were covered with maintenance-free, high-tech wood. Between the façade and the wood covering are pots filled with boxwood balls that run along the whole of the perimeter of this showcase balcony. The living and dining rooms have encroached on the balcony, using two fixed glass cubes.

SMALL BALCONY

Maximizing the outdoor space of an apartment with a gabled roof — charming but very small — put the designer's ingenuity to the test. Solutions included preventing any distortion of the passage with a fixed-arm parasol fastened to the façade. This is also a great idea for an area without the room for a larger awning. This white corner is composed of a pair of easy chairs and a modern sofa made from a material suitable for the outdoors. It is completed with a small coffee table and plant pots with plants and palm trees to add a paradise-island touch to this urban ambiance. Beside it is a dining area with a table, two chairs and a bench. To make the most of the available space, the area is illuminated with a floor lamp, essential if you want to avoid overhead lights.

FLOOR TREATMENT: BRAZILIAN WALNUT FLOORING | PLANT POTS AND PLANTER BOXES: CERAMIC-LOOK PLASTIC POTS | OUTDOOR FURNITURE: ROTOMOLDED POLYETHYLENE EASY CHAIRS AND SOFA, COFFEE TABLE, TABLE WITH POLYETHYLENE BARS FOR THE TOP AND A STAINLESS STEEL BASE, CHAIRS AND BENCH FROM THE SAME COLLECTION | PLANT SPECIES: PALM TREES AND AROMATIC PLANTS | DECORATIVE OBJECTS: FLOOR LAMP, POLISHED METAL BUCKETS AND VASES

The sloping ground was evened out with Brazilian walnut flooring, the same material used to build the narrow bench that runs along one side of the balcony. The décor is modern and playful, involving white tones and contemporary furniture which, together with the parasol and palm trees, give the terrace an Ibiza look in stark contrast with the environment and the tiles on the roof of the building.

IN SEARCH OF PRIVACY

THE LOCATION OF THIS BALCONY ON A NOISY, LOW-FLOOR CITY APARTMENT COMPLETELY CONDITIONED ANY REDESIGN WORK TO MAKE IT AS QUIET AND PRIVATE AS POSSIBLE. The ground was leveled with a flooring of the same wood used to cover the deep planter box that runs around the front railing of the balcony. The air-conditioning unit was concealed with timber boards that form a vent at the front to achieve a harmonious vision of the whole. The folding off-white awnings are particularly important in this space, both because of their size and the material which screens the balcony from passersby and lets the abundant light in while also filtering it. A custom-designed sofa made from the same Brazilian walnut wood seems to emerge from the floor between two side tables.

FLOOR TREATMENT: BRAZILIAN WALNUT FLOORING | **PLANT POTS AND PLANTER BOXES:** WOOD USED TO COVER THE ELONGATED ORIGINAL PLANTER BOX OF THE FAÇADE, AND TERRACCOTTA | **OUTDOOR FURNITURE:** BENCH-CUM-SOFA BETWEEN TWO CUSTOM-MADE SIDE TABLES IN THE ONE PIECE, DECK CHAIR AND TRUNK | **PLANT SPECIES:** FICUS BENJAMINA, MYOPORUM AND CRASSULAS | **DECORATIVE OBJECTS:** WHITE UPHOLSTERED SQUARE CUSHIONS ON THE BENCH, THROW PILLOWS, OUTDOOR CUBE LAMPS, WICKER BASKET

The balance between this landscaped balcony and the inside of the home comes from the five-seat sofa that emerges from the covering of the railing and faces the house. The custom-made planter boxes that enclose the balcony in the façade are exposed at either end of the balcony and their curved shape adds dynamism.

OVERSIZING THE INTERIOR

The tiny dimensions of this elongated balcony with no initial charm made it difficult to try to develop the outdoor space, so the idea instead was to prolong the indoor area. This simple solution has expanded the property, integrating both ambiances through a play of depths. The glass wall of the living-cum-dining room allows generous views from this space that opens onto the exterior, converted into a beautiful showcase for the view and to live in. The timber floor extends up the railing of the balcony and is wider at the top to form a long planter box of ficus benjamina. These and a number of very transparent screens block the space from the street. A timber structure that further insulates this warm and agreeable area has been positioned next to the adjacent building.

FLOOR TREATMENT: WOOD FLOORING | PLANT POTS AND PLANTER BOXES: WOOD AND TERRACOTTA AMPHORAE | OUTDOOR FURNITURE: BENCH, TABLE AND FOLDING CHAIRS, EASY CHAIR | PLANT SPECIES: FICUS BENJAMINA | DECORATIVE OBJECTS: CUSHIONS, FRUIT DISH, FLOWER POTS, METAL CUBE AND FLOOR LAMP

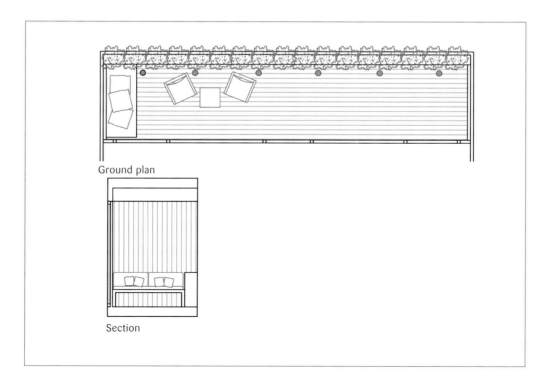

Ground plan

Section

This balcony, in front of the property's living areas, has been converted into an extension of the living room and an outdoor showcase for the apartment. It features an easy chair and a small bench/sofa that extends from the living room. A small table and folding chairs with a metal base and timber seats and backs have been positioned as a complement to the main dining room. The opaque bubble glass from the original façade and through which natural light enters has been concealed with a plant that climbs up from a terracotta amphora.

COURTYARDS AND GARDENS

A DINING ROOM IN THE COURTYARD

THIS HOUSE IN THE MIDDLE OF THE CITY HAS A COURTYARD AS WIDE AS THE FACADE — AROUND 16 FEET — AND IS FAIRLY LONG. UNTIL NOW IT WAS QUITE DULL AND DID NOT HAVE ANY PARTICULAR USE. Just a few essential elements were used to make it into a spacious dining area for guests and to get around the handicap of its unusual floor design. From the doorway of the property, stairs lead down to the meeting area with Brazilian walnut flooring the width of the staircase and with a large square table with eight chairs. The sides have been landscaped and between the plants and the flooring two white stone paths created that add new depth and brightness to the space. A number of partitions were built for a canvas awning that protects the dining area.

FLOOR TREATMENT: BRAZILIAN WALNUT FLOORING AND WHITE STONES | OUTDOOR FURNITURE: SQUARE DINING TABLE, EIGHT CHAIRS AND A LOW BENCH | PLANT SPECIES: BAMBOO PLANTS, LEMON TREES, PARKINSONIA | DECORATIVE OBJECTS: WALL APPLIQUES AND FLOOR HALOGEN LIGHTS TO ILLUMINATE THE TREES

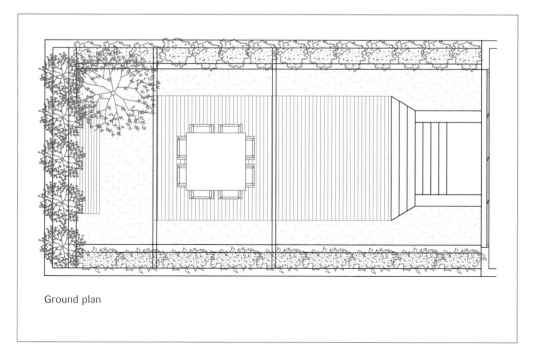

Ground plan

To increase privacy, low walls were built from wooden boards separating the space from the house next door and the street. Given its particular function as a summer dining area, a canvas awning was positioned using partitions. Between the flooring and the perimeter planter boxes, the white stones confer different profundities on the space and stop it from looking like a long corridor. At the end of the courtyard, a small bench can be used to hold the utensils needed at mealtimes.

BUSINESS CENTER

This garden is found in a business centre in the Eixample district of Barcelona. Its initial state – a typical communal-block courtyard completely lacking in charm or use – was transformed into a multi-purpose zone for relaxing in after lengthy business meetings, an oasis that emerges from the balance between the thick vegetation and the modern living spaces. Flooring leads to the Club zone, with a coffee table and chairs, supported on another section of flooring superimposed on the first and distinguished by the change of position of the planks. The rest of the original terrazzo was covered with crushed stones and various plants in the pots that decorate the garden. Of note are the leafy ficus benjamina and the lemon tree that hides the air-conditioning units, surrounded by a landscaped area with a bench.

FLOOR TREATMENT: BRAZILIAN WALNUT FLOORING AND CRUSHED STONES | PLANT POTS AND PLANTER BOXES: TERRACOTTA AND WOOD | OUTDOOR FURNITURE: TABLE WITH ALUMINUM BASE AND SOLID TOP, ALUMINUM CHAIRS WITH BATYLINE SEAT AND BACK AND TEAK BENCH | PLANT SPECIES: FICUS BENJAMINA, BOXWOOD, LEMON TREE | DECORATIVE OBJECTS: VASES, CUSHIONS AND BASKETS

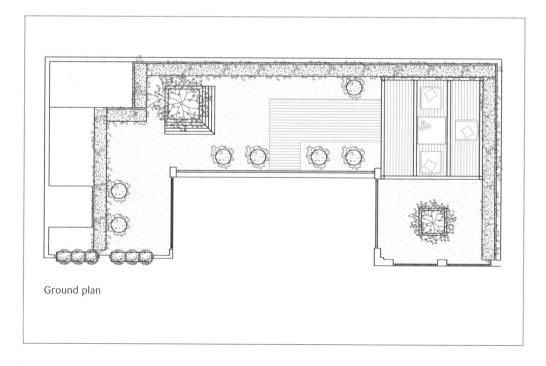

Ground plan

AROMATIC GARDEN

This terrace pertains to a ground-floor apartment where the owner wanted to create an outdoor living area surrounded by aromatic plants. Because of its location, the first job was to raise the wall with a timber fence that runs around the whole perimeter to ensure privacy. Two open areas determine the functionality of each space: a small living area with a low side table and a pair of chairs and further on, a spacious dining space that can seat up to eight people. A pair of awnings that overhang from the façade shield the living and dining areas from the sun. In terms of the gardening work, one very important aspect in this project was that everything had to revolve around Mediterranean aromatic plants, the colors and scents of which were used to create a very special ambiance.

FLOOR TREATMENT: ORIGINAL TERRAZZO | **PLANT POTS AND PLANTER BOXES:** ZINC AND EARTHENWARE | **OUTDOOR FURNITURE:** DINING TABLE AND SIDE TABLES WITH TEAK TOPS AND ALUMINUM BASES, CHAIRS WITH THE BACK AND SEAT COVERED IN SPECIAL OUTDOOR FABRIC | **PLANT SPECIES:** GROUPS OF LAVENDER, LAUREL, THYME AND SANTOLINA | **DECORATIVE OBJECTS:** BASKETS, BOWLS, TABLE RUNNER

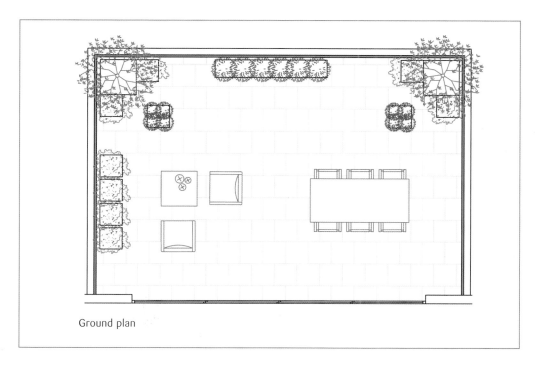

Ground plan

The sense of symmetry comes from the arrangement of the plant pots: in both outdoor corners, three groups of square, black zinc pots filled with the same group of plants behind small earthenware pots that grow thyme. The same idea was used in the long and low earthenware planter box. The furniture is as delicate as the aromatic and Mediterranean garden design: delicate tables and chairs define the function of a pleasantly simple and effective space.

SMOOTH TRANSITIONS

THIS IS THE BACK COURTYARD OF A GROUND-FLOOR APARTMENT WHERE THE OWNER WANTED TO GAIN THREE AREAS: A DINING SPACE, A GARDEN AND A COVERED STUDY WITH DIVERSE FUNCTIONS. The topographic conditions meant the different ambiances had to be layered, as it was a sunken courtyard with a profound height difference with regards the house. To make the transitions smooth, pinewood flooring was installed at two heights and the height difference regulated by the use of 7-inch-high steps, only possible in outdoor areas. At the top is a small dining area with a lateral-arm awning, then comes an intermediate terrace with large pot plants, followed by a diaphanous garden with a grass bed, and at the end a studio made from pinewood with a sliding door and a fixed glass wall.

FLOOR TREATMENT: TREATED PINEWOOD FLOORING AND GRASS | PLANT POTS AND PLANTER BOXES: LARGE BLACK ZINC POT PLANTS | OUTDOOR FURNITURE: TABLE WITH ALUMINUM STRUCTURE AND WOODEN BOARDS FOR THE TOP; ALUMINUM CHAIRS WITH SCREEN-FABRIC BACKS AND SEATS | PLANT SPECIES: PERENNIAL LEAF CALIFORNIA PEPPER TREE, JASMINE, NATURAL GRASS AND LAVENDER PLANTS | DECORATIVE OBJECTS: CANDLE LAMP, TABLE RUNNER, BOWLS AND PLATTER

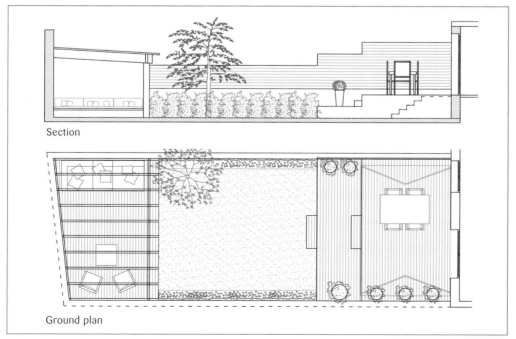

Section

Ground plan

LANDSCAPED PASSAGEWAY

This passageway that leads to the entrance of an ophthalmology clinic used to be the path to the building's service staircase. For the purpose of the renovation work, i.e., to add charisma and provide the clinic with a main access, one striking solution lay in installing a laminated glass and iron pergola to protect the passageway from the rain. It is a floating structure, as the narrow space made it necessary to eliminate every obstacle and also determined that only one side of the passageway would be planted with large carob trees in planter boxes. Between them, white crushed stones add light and outdoor spotlights illuminate the path at night. At the end, a change in the flooring highlights the waiting area, with Brazilian walnut boards, an L-shaped bench, creepers and bamboo.

FLOOR TREATMENT: ORIGINAL TERRAZZO AND BRAZILIAN WALNUT FLOORING | PLANT POTS AND PLANTER BOXES: RAILWAY SLEEPERS | OUTDOOR FURNITURE: GARDEN SHED AND BENCH | PLANT SPECIES: CAROB TREES, CREEPERS AND BAMBOOS | DECORATIVE OBJECTS: METAL BASKETS AND CUBES, POT PLANT COVERS

PLAY OF SUPERIMPOSITIONS

This project involved the terrace of a family home attached to the owner's brother's house. Because of that and to completely separate the houses, a low, gapped-timber fence makes a subtle border. The simple and practical play of volumes and superimpositions makes for a peaceful setting that conveys balance. To avoid using high-maintenance grass, a river of white marble stones was made, from which wooden flooring that delimits the dining area and extends to the house protrudes. At one end, a custom-designed planter box with flower bed (which breaks the predominant colors of green, brown and white) and a tree stand out for being positioned higher than the other levels. A bamboo wall ensures the privacy of the courtyard.

FLOOR TREATMENT: BRAZILIAN WALNUT FLOORING AND WHITE MARBLE STONES | PLANT POTS AND PLANTER BOXES: BLACK ZINC POTS AND CUSTOM-DESIGNED PLANTER BOXES | OUTDOOR FURNITURE: TABLE WITH A STEEL BASE AND TIMBER TOP AND SIX OUTDOOR CHAIRS | PLANT SPECIES: BAMBOO, FLOWERS, BOXWOOD AND AN OLIVE TREE | DECORATIVE OBJECTS: DINNER SERVICE AND GLASS VASES

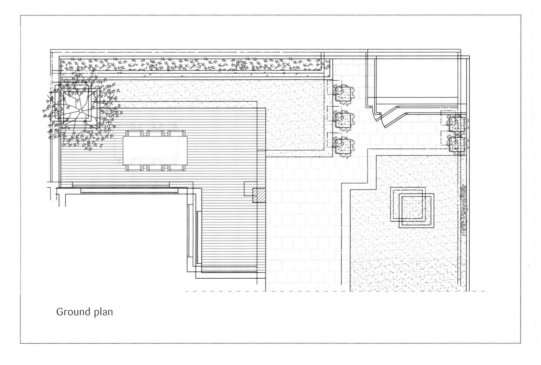

Ground plan

WELCOMING SUMMER DINING AREA

THIS TERRACE BELONGS TO THE GROUND-FLOOR APARTMENT OF A LARGE BUILDING, WHOSE BRIGHT, WHITE MARBLE FACING AND ABUNDANT ENTRY OF LIGHT CONDITIONED THE DECORATION. This square space is used as a summer dining area for the home and was fitted with Brazilian walnut flooring, the same material used for the pots filled with Mediterranean plants that run along the whole of the perimeter. To make the most of this welcoming space, the inside walls were painted a brick-red color. This tone was also chosen for the fabric of a parasol attached to the façade and whose fully adjustable, extendible arm enables it to move effortlessly and adds a flexible service to the whole of the terrace. These solutions were able to tone down the excess of light.

FLOOR TREATMENT: BRAZILIAN WALNUT FLOORING | PLANT POTS AND PLANTER BOXES: BRAZILIAN WALNUT | OUTDOOR FURNITURE: TABLE WITH MARBLE TOP AND BLACK-PAINTED FORGED-IRON LEGS, ALUMINUM AND TEAK CHAIRS | PLANT SPECIES: LEMON TREE, OLIVE TREE AND MEDITERRANEAN PLANTS | DECORATIVE OBJECTS: WICKER COFFEE TABLE AND A PAIR OF SMALL PLANT POTS

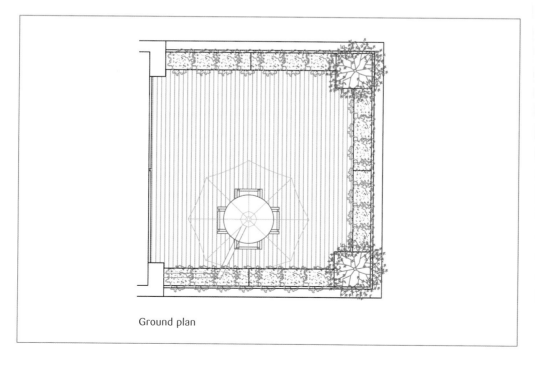

Ground plan

To keep the central space uncluttered and able to accommodate the round table and four chairs, a perimeter planter box was used which makes the area look brighter. The Brazilian walnut planter boxes maintain continuity with the floor and the harmonious feel of the whole. The walls were painted the same brick-red tone as the material of the parasol, whose adjustable arm, dimensions and mobility protect this square terrace perfectly.

OUTDOOR SMOKING AREA

THIS COURTYARD BELONGS TO THE STUDIO OF A RENOWNED FASHION DESIGNER. It is on the top floor, in the showroom and private fashion-parade area, and is used as a relaxation space for the models, employees, clients and guests when they step out for a cigarette. It has also been designed as a showcase for the indoor spaces. An outdoor smoking area was designed in which white marble stones boost the natural light and a Brazilian walnut runway expand into a space with benches, ash trays and plants. The vegetation – a species of mandarin tree and box-wood balls – composes an excellent view for the interior stages. The runway is illuminated with appliqué lights along the length and makes for a pleasing atmosphere when the light falls.

FLOOR TREATMENT: BRAZILIAN WALNUT FLOORING AND WHITE MARBLE STONES | PLANT POTS AND PLANTER BOXES: ITALIAN CERAMIC POTS | OUTDOOR FURNITURE: CUSTOM-MADE TROPICAL WOOD BENCHES | PLANT SPECIES: BOXWOOD BALLS AND KUMQUAT TREES | DECORATIVE OBJECTS: CERAMIC AND WICKER TRAYS, ASH TRAYS AND LIGHTS EMBEDDED IN THE RUNWAY